Healthy Eating

Fruit and Vegetables

Susan Martineau
and Hel James

W
FRANKLIN WATTS
LONDON • SYDNEY

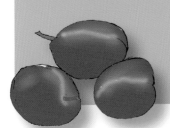

An Appleseed Editions book

First published in 2006 by
Franklin Watts
338 Euston Road
London NWI 3BH

Franklin Watts Australia
Hachette Children's Books
Level 17/207 Kent Street
Sydney NSW 2000

Created by Appleseed Editions Ltd,
Well House, Friars Hill, Guestling, East Sussex TN35 4ET

Designed and illustrated by Helen James
Edited by Jinny Johnson

634

ISBN-10: 0-7496-6722-2
ISBN-13: 978-0-7496-6722-1
Dewey Classification: 641.3' 03

A CIP catalogue for this book is available from the British Library

Photographs: 11 Owaki-Kulla/Corbis; 12-13 Patrick Johns/Corbis; 14 Hel James; 15 Michael Pole/Corbis;
16 Douglas Peebles/Corbis; 17 Peter Turnley/Corbis; 19 Michael Boys/Corbis; 21 Steve Terrill/Corbis;
23 Eric Crichton/Corbis; 24 Richard Morrell/Corbis; 26 Daniel Boschung/Zefa/Corbis; 29 PhotoCuisine/Corbis.
Front cover: Ed Young/Corbis

Printed and bound in Thailand

Contents

Food for health   4

A balanced plateful!   6

Vital vitamins and magic minerals   8

Fantastic fruit   10

Apples, pears and plums   12

Berries and grapes   14

Tropical fruit   16

Vegetables galore   18

Fruit vegetables   20

Pods and seeds   22

Vegetables under the ground   24

A bowl of salad   26

Loads of lentils   28

Words to remember   30

Index and websites   32

Food for health

Our bodies are like amazing machines.
Just like machines, we need the right
sort of fuel to give us energy and
to keep us working properly.

If we don't eat the kind of food we need to keep us healthy we may become ill or feel tired and grumpy. Our bodies don't really like it if we eat too much of one sort of food, like cakes or chips.

We need a balanced diet. That means eating different sorts of good food in the right amounts.

You'll be surprised at how much there is to know about where our food comes from and why some kinds of food are better for us than others. Finding out about food is great fun and very tasty!

What's so good about fruit and vegetables?

Eating at least five different fruits and vegetables every day helps to keep you healthy.

A balanced plateful!

The good things or nutrients our bodies need come from different kinds of food. Let's have a look at what your plate should have on it. It all looks delicious!

Rice, bread and pasta

These foods contain carbohydrates and they give us energy. About a third of our food should come from this group.

Fruit and vegetables

Rice, bread and pasta

Bread, cheese and salad gives you carbohydrates, protein, vitamins and minerals.

Fruit and vegetables

These are full of great vitamins and minerals and fibre and they help keep you healthy. About a third of our food should come from this group.

Milk, yogurt and cheese

These dairy foods give us protein and also calcium to make strong bones and teeth.

Meat, fish and eggs

Protein from these helps your body grow and repair itself. They are body-building foods and we need to eat them every day.

Sugar and fats

We only need small amounts of these. Too much can be bad for our teeth and make us fat.

Milk, yogurt and cheese

Sugar and fats

Meat, fish and eggs

Water

We need to drink at least 6 glasses of water every day.

Vital vitamins and magic minerals

Fruit and vegetables give us all sorts of wonderful vitamins and minerals. These help us grow well and stay healthy. Fruit and vegetables also give us fibre. Fibre keeps our digestive system working properly.

High five!

Try to eat five portions of fruit and vegetables every day. Choose different ones so you have a great balance of vitamins and minerals. There are lots of different kinds of delicious fruit and vegetable so it's easy to eat even more than that!

Super-charged menu

Breakfast

Have some fresh fruit on your cereal.

Super-charged menu

Lunch

Put some salad in your lunchbox!

You can get fresh, frozen or tinned vegetables.

Super-charged menu

Dinner

Munch some carrots and broccoli with your evening meal.

Fantastic fruit

Fruit grows on trees, bushes and plants. All flowering plants have seeds. The fleshy fruit is what forms round the seeds to protect them. How many different sorts of fruits can you think of? Have they got lots of little seeds or one big one like a stone?

Oranges and lemons

Oranges, lemons and limes are called citrus fruits. Other citrus fruits are satsumas, mandarins, clementines and grapefruit. They all grow on trees. The pips inside them are the seeds of the trees.

Lemon

Orange

Lime

Freshly squeezed fruit juice is packed with vitamins.

Grapefruit

Oranges are picked and put into big tubs. Then they go to a packing house to be checked, washed and labelled.

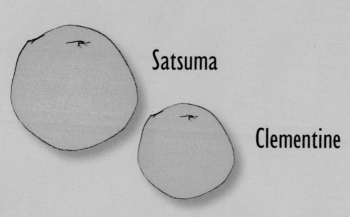

Satsuma

Clementine

Citrus fruits are full of Vitamin C. This helps to keep the body strong to fight off illness.

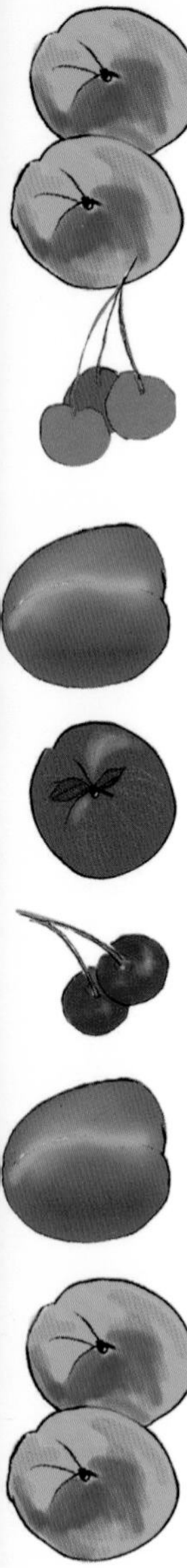

Apples, pears and plums

Apples and pears are hard fruits with small seeds inside them. Plums have just one large stone in the middle. Other fruits with one big stone are nectarines, peaches, apricots and cherries. All these fruits grow on trees.

Snack on some delicious cherries but watch out for the stones!

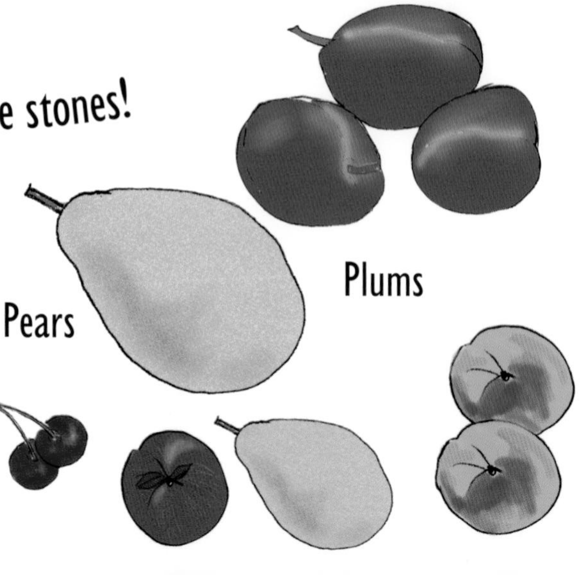

Pears

Plums

Apples have to be picked by hand because machines would bruise them. They are washed and then stored in cold buildings to keep them fresh.

Make a juicy fruit salad with all your favourite fruits.

When you eat one of these delicious fruits you are giving your body all sorts of helpful nutrients and fibre. Peaches, nectarines and apricots have loads of Vitamin A in them. Vitamin A is really good for your eyes.

Berries and grapes

Strawberries, raspberries, blueberries and blackberries are all loaded with Vitamin C. Berries are delicious eaten just as they are. They can also be mixed into yogurts or cooked to make jam.

Grapes grow in big bunches on long, trailing plants called vines. You can get green or black grapes. Some grapes are dried to make raisins.

Strawberries

Raspberries

Blueberries

Blackberries

Cut a kiwi in half and scoop out the sweet green flesh and seeds. This gives you all the Vitamin C your body needs for a whole day.

Kiwi fruit look like brown furry eggs. They also grow on a plant like a vine.

Find out if there is a farm near you where you can pick your own berries. How about making some jam?

Blackcurrants

Tropical fruit

Bananas, pineapples and mangoes grow in tropical countries. It is hot and sunny all year round there with lots of rain, so just right for growing these fruits. Try to find out about other tropical fruits such as papayas and lychees. See how many of them you can spot in your local shops.

Mangoes grow on trees and have a large, flat stone inside their sweet orange flesh. A ripe mango is a delicious treat full of Vitamins C and A.

Bananas grow on very large plants that look like trees. Many bunches, or hands, of bananas grow on the plant. They are picked when they are still green.

The bananas are checked and labelled before being packed into boxes. Then the bananas are carried by ship to different parts of the world. They are kept in huge fridges to keep them fresh on the journey.

How many fruits can you find in my hat?

Vegetables galore

A vegetable is any part of a plant that can be eaten. It can be the leaves, stalks, buds or roots of a plant. There are lots of delicious vegetables to choose from. You could ask all your friends to name their favourite one to find out which one is top veg!

Eat your greens!

Green vegetables really are good for you. They have all sorts of great nutrients and fibre in them.

Cauliflower is in the same vegetable family as broccoli and cabbage.

Broccoli is the flower bud of the plant it grows on.

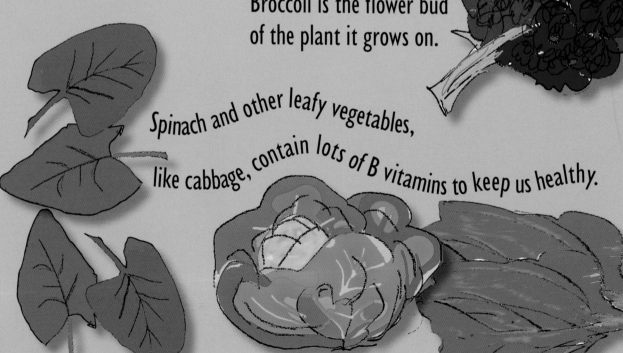

Spinach and other leafy vegetables, like cabbage, contain lots of B vitamins to keep us healthy.

Fruit vegetables

Some vegetables are called fruit vegetables.
They have juicy flesh and come in all sorts
of vitamin-packed shapes, sizes and colours.

Tomatoes, peppers and aubergines grow on small bushes. In cooler countries farmers grow them in large glass houses called greenhouses.

Avocados grow on trees and look a bit like pears. They are full of vitamins and minerals.

Cucumbers, marrows, courgettes and pumpkins are all in the same vegetable family. They grow on trailing bushes or vines.

Aubergines and peppers

Avocado

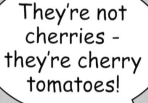
They're not cherries - they're cherry tomatoes!

Cucumber

Tomatoes are tasty little packages of Vitamin C.

Pumpkins are lovely made
into a golden soup.

21

Pods and seeds

French beans, runner beans and mangetout (or snow peas) are all pods. They grow on climbing plants. We can cook and eat the whole pod including the little beans or peas inside them.

Peas grow inside pods. It's fun to take the peas out of their pods, but in factories there is a special machine called a viner to do this.

Frozen peas

Peas and other vegetables are often frozen before being sold in the shops. They are frozen as soon as they are picked so that they keep all their good vitamins inside them.

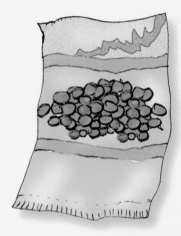

Corn on the cob

Sweetcorn is the seeds of a grass plant called maize. We can eat the seeds, or kernels, straight off the cob they grow on.

22

It's easy to grow your own runner beans.

Did you know that popcorn is made out of corn kernels?

Pea pod and peas

Vegetables
under the ground

Potatoes, carrots, beetroot and parsnips are all vegetables that grow under the ground. They are called root vegetables. They give us lots of vitamins and fibre. Carrots are full of Vitamin A.

Potatoes are dug up by machines. The farmer checks through them and takes out any bad ones.

Beetroot

Parsnips

Carrots

What about organic veg?

Vegetable growers often use special chemicals to kill bugs and weeds and make the vegetables grow better. Some people think these chemicals are bad for us and they also harm the environment. Organic vegetables are grown without using chemicals.

Chips?

Baked potato?

Potatoes can be boiled, mashed, baked or made into chips and crisps. Chips and crisps are cooked in lots of fat so they are not the healthiest way to eat potatoes.

A bowl of salad

You can make a salad with all sorts of lettuce leaves. You can also use baby spinach leaves or watercress. They taste quite strong so it is nice to mix them with other leaves too.

Pots of herbs

Herbs add a nice taste to all kinds of meals. You could grow your own in pots on a windowsill.

Basil smells wonderful and is used to make a delicious sauce called pesto that tastes great on pasta.

Mint is good with lamb dishes or with vegetables like potatoes or peas.

Curly parsley

Parsley can be sprinkled on top of dishes or added to soups and stews.

Flat-leaf parsley

Have a salad with your supper or snack on a bowl of raw vegetables. Try carrot sticks, radishes and celery. They are delicious in your lunchbox too.

Loads of lentils

Lentils, chickpeas and different kinds of beans are the dried seeds of bean and pea plants. These dried seeds are called pulses. They keep for months and are great for making soups, curries and stews.

Pulses are full of protein and so good for vegetarians who do not get protein from meat. They also contain iron and fibre. Soya beans can be made into bean curd, or tofu.

Beanburger

Beans on toast

Chilli con carne

Bring on the beans!

Baked beans in tins are very good for you. They are made out of dried haricot beans and tomato sauce. But try to find the ones with 'low sugar' and 'low salt' on the label.

Chickpea stew

Red lentils

Split peas

Borlotti beans

Cannellini beans

Chickpeas

Kidney beans

Puy lentils

Soya beans

Corn

Words to remember

calcium   A mineral which helps build healthy bones and teeth. Watercress and broccoli have calcium in them.

carbohydrates   Starches and sugars in food that give us energy. Carbohydrate foods are rice, pasta, bread and potatoes. Bananas have carbohydrate in them and so they give us lots of energy too.

chemicals   Chemicals are substances that can be used for all sorts of things. Some, called pesticides, are used to kill weeds and bugs in fields.

citrus fruits   Fruits like oranges, lemons, limes and grapefruit. They have a thick skin and juicy flesh.

digestive system   The parts of your body where your food gets broken down and turned into energy and nutrients.

environment   The world around us.

fibre   Fibre is found in plant foods like grains and vegetables. It helps our insides, our digestive system, to work properly.

iron   A mineral in food that we need to keep our blood healthy.

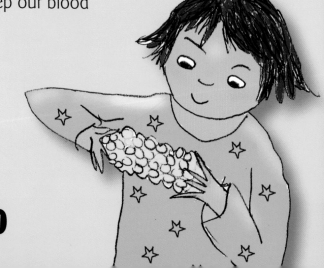

minerals   Nutrients in food that help our bodies work properly. Calcium and iron are minerals.

nutrients   Parts of food that your body needs for energy, to grow healthily and to repair itself.

organic   Organic fruit and vegetables are grown without using chemicals to kill weeds and bugs and to make the vegetables grow better.

protein   Body-building food that makes our bodies grow well and stay healthy.

tofu   This is also called bean curd and is a cheese-like food made out of soya beans.

vines   Long, trailing plants. Grapes and kiwi fruit grow on vines.

vitamins   Nutrients in food that help our bodies work properly:

vitamin A   This vitamin is in most dark green or yellow fruits and vegetables. It helps to keep us healthy and especially looks after our eyes.

B vitamins   B vitamins help turn our food into energy and keep our muscles, skin and blood healthy. B Vitamins have special names like folate, niacin and thiamin. (If you see these on a label you know the food has B Vitamins in it.) Green leafy vegetables contain folate.

vitamin C   Keeps our gums and teeth healthy, mends cuts and bruises and makes us strong to fight off infection and illness. Our bodies cannot store Vitamin C so we need some every day.

Index

apples 12-13

balanced diet 4, 6-7
bananas 16-17
berries 14-15

citrus fruits 10-11

fruit 10-11, 12-13, 14-15, 16-17
fruit vegetables 20-21

grapes 14
green vegetables 18-19

herbs 26

kiwi 15

mangoes 16
minerals 8

oranges 10-11

peas and beans 22-23
pulses 28-29

root vegetables 24-25

salad 26-27
soya beans 28-29, 31

vitamin A 13, 24, 31
vitamin C 11, 14-15, 20, 31
vitamins 8, 31

WEBSITES

General food information for all ages
www.bbc.co.uk/health/healthy_living/nutrition

Food Standards Agency – healthy eating, food labelling
www.eatwell.gov.uk

Quizzes and games on food
www.coolfoodplanet.org

Information and games on healthy eating
www.lifebytes.gov.uk/eating/eat_menu.html

Worksheets and activities
www.foodforum.org.uk

Practical advice on healthy eating
www.fitness.org.uk